THE EVERYDAY HERO

DELIA STEINBERG GUZMÁN

First published in Spanish under the title *El Héroe Cotidiano*, 1996.
Translated from Spanish by Julian Scott.
Re-designed for English edition by Janki Shah, Neha Mehta.

Published in 2018 by

NEW ACROPOLIS

New Acropolis Cultural Organization.
Mumbai, India.

www.acropolis.org.in
info@acropolis.org.in

Copyright © New Acropolis Cultural Organization 2018.
All Rights Reserved. No part of this book may be reproduced or transmitted in any form by any means, electronic or mechanical, including photocopying or recording, or by any information storage and retrieval system, except as may be expressly permitted in writing by the publisher.

ISBN: 978-81-920193-6-9

Printed in India.

THE EVERYDAY HERO

DELIA STEINBERG GUZMÁN

Table of Contents

7	Foreword
9	New Age, Old Science
13	Crisis
17	The Cancer of Separatism
21	The Pathology of Fear
23	Facing Disaster
25	Reclaiming Courage
27	Pain and Suffering
31	Stress
35	Aggression
39	Fear of Public Opinion
41	Is it Worth it?
43	Knowledge or Wisdom?
45	The Need to Stand Out

49	What is Inspiration?
51	Why do Feelings get Worn Out?
55	The Everyday Hero
57	Criticism
59	Symbolic Language
63	Being Free
67	Time
69	Eros, Love
73	Mistrust
77	What We Love and What We Fear
79	A Fulfilling Life
83	For the Brave
85	The Eternal Seeker
87	We Propose…
91	Self-Confidence
93	Swimming Against the Current
97	In the Classical Tradition

Foreword

Dear Reader,

You are holding a treasure in your hands.

When speaking of treasure, what usually comes to mind is the gold chest of legends.

But there are other more intangible types of treasure, which make their possessor no less rich, and maybe even more so.

These are the treasures of the soul.

Delia Steinberg Guzmán is a philosopher and a poet, and she makes music with her words.

With her sensitivity, observation and compassion she weaves reflective articles around the themes of our lives. Her ideas resonate within the chambers of the heart and echo later in moments of unexpected inspiration, sowing new seeds of understanding.

This is not a book to read once or twice, but one to keep close, to read again and again, as we discover ourselves changing from one reading to the other.

This is a book for those who dare to be Everyday Heroes.

Greatness, after all, is only for the few. But while not all of us can be great, all of us can be *good*, which is in itself a challenge worth fighting for.

All of us can be heroes, everyday heroes, who break their self-imposed limitations, to offer something meaningful to this world and to make it a little better.

And as a great philosopher once said: "Every step we take towards the good within us is somehow a step taken by all humanity."

Have an inspiring read,

Gilad Sommer.
Director of *New Acropolis Chicago*.

New Age, Old Science

It has often been said and written that we are living in the age of technology, and we are constantly reminded of all the advantages that this implies.

All our activities are systematized; electronic computing extends to all aspects of life; human labour is being taken over by machines every day; communications reduce distances and time. In short, we are told that we are on the point of attaining the paradise so often dreamed of, with plenty of free time every day and several days off every week.

But to the many paradoxes of our present times another very striking one should be added.

Technology has tried to make all aspects of material life easier, but nothing has been done to benefit our psychological, mental and spiritual life; these subjective worlds continue to be as disorganized as they were in the age of the cave dwellers.

It may be objected that psychology, and other sciences that are auxiliary to it, have classified the human being into different types, making it easier to recognize them and, in the case of illness, to treat them. This is true; but classifying human types in textbooks and charts does nothing to resolve the practical problem of human beings who are defenceless against themselves. To know that we are shy is not equivalent to curing shyness; to know that we have an out of control imagination does not help us to master it either.

Today human beings can work with an immense diversity of machines, but are incapable of dealing with a psychological depression, or of moderating their instincts, restraining their anger or awakening their spirituality. And it is not that they don't want to do these things; they would often like to do so, but they can't. They don't know how to. Technology has not taken an interest in these problems, nor has it been capable of coming up with any system that would allow us to work with those subjective unknown quantities of the inner human being.

As a result, while science and technology are advancing hand in hand, making ever more futuristic plans for greater material comfort, human beings are sinking ever more deeply into the despair of their unsatisfied selves. The more free time they have, the more afraid they feel; because they don't know how to be alone with themselves, they don't understand the hidden driving forces of that strange companion they live with every day, their inner Self.

Instead of providing the real service for which they were designed, machines have usurped the powers of human beings, they have enslaved the very being they were intended to liberate. We can hardly even imagine a life today without watches, telephones, electrical devices, elevators, escalators or televisions. And the human being hides away in a corner, useless in the face of the very technology he has created.

People talk of the systematization of data, but they cannot organize their inner life.

They talk of stopping pollution, but they cannot avoid bad thoughts and feelings.

They talk of supersonic aeroplanes, but they cannot accelerate mental understanding.

They talk of peace and love, and of human rights, but they don't know how to love one another or how to live in peace; they don't understand human rights, for the simple reason that they don't understand the human being.

Technology? Liberation? Mastery of life? Let us leave aside paradoxes and realize once and for all that only someone who is an expert in the difficult and marvellous art of self-knowledge can give value to freedom and life, and can make use of science and technology for the benefit of humanity.

Let us begin, then, the NEW AGE of the OLD SCIENCE, the science of "KNOW THYSELF".

Crisis

The old idea that the classical Greeks had of "crisis" is more relevant than ever today. Whether or not we want to accept it, we are evidently in crisis, which means that we are at a time of change, at a turning point where the angle of history is facing in two directions.

In times of crisis, in other words, in times of change, all things tend to appear unstable; insecurity and doubt are the order of the day and no one wants to risk great undertakings because of the uncertainty of what may happen tomorrow.

It is in these moments of crisis that human beings are most likely to become confrontational, with no room for negotiation.

There is bitter opposition between those who are on one side of change or the other: those who look back at what is being left behind and those who dream of what is to come in the future. Each one has good and more than adequate arguments to defend their position; and each one defends it with the methods that are typical of times of crisis: violence and a lack of understanding for the other.

Those who look to the past with nostalgia are disparagingly called "reactionaries". They are harshly criticized for not fully embracing the adventure of the future. But they do not feel reactionary; they are simply trying not to waste all the experience that has been gained and to make use of it. They are trying to store up memories and knowledge from the past like someone who accumulates wealth so as to be able to live better in the future.

Those who look only towards the future – which, incidentally, they do not yet know – are disparagingly called "revolutionaries". For them, none of humanity's past experiences are useful any more and there is only constant change, a total break with everything old and a worship of what is assumed to be better because it is new. But they do not feel like revolutionaries in the destructive sense of the word; they have just found that none of the solutions proposed so far has brought humanity the happiness it aspires to; so they think that the solution must lie in something different from what has been known until now and that all the old formulas must therefore be set aside as unworkable.

At times of crisis, however, at the turning points of history, it is difficult to see things clearly. Those on either side of the argument become obsessed with their own particular views and can contribute nothing to a harmonious solution.

In moments of crisis, we propose taking the geometric figure of the angle as a model, with its two legs facing in different directions, but joined at the top to give a higher meaning and purpose.

There are, of course, some worn out and outdated elements from the past which have been proven by failure to be invalid and unusable; but in the past there is also an accumulation of rich experience that could help us to replicate successes and avoid failures.

In the soil of the future, the glories to come are no doubt already growing and developing, and we cannot ignore them, because we are all walking towards them; but this is not the same as accepting without question that everything in the future will be better just because it is different.

Although it is true that we are in crisis, this will not last forever. Change is renewal: it means to use the old and powerful columns of the past as a basis on which to build the beautiful capitals of the present. This is the only way we will construct the edifice of history.

The Cancer of Separatism

When we argued some years ago in our writings and lectures that a new Middle Ages was approaching, the prediction seemed exaggerated and almost fatalistic.

We also explained at the time that the repetition of historical cycles did not necessarily have to be seen as a calamity or regression, but as part of the natural course of life, which progresses gradually in a circular and spiral-shaped manner, touching similar points along the way, although at different levels of evolution.

Far from being fatalistic, let alone exaggerated, events today are proving the truth of those words. Now there are a great many authors and scholars who are talking about the phenomenon of a medieval period resulting from the last few centuries of our history, as a period of rest and recovery before a possible "renaissance".

There are various characteristics that indicate the presence of an intermediate cycle for our civilization. But there is one which is particularly relevant today, due to the serious complications it may bring if we fail to realize its true magnitude. I am talking about separatism.

Beyond its political meanings – although these are also included – separatism is a force that infiltrates all human expressions with a tendency to dissolve everything that has been achieved until now. It leads one cell to oppose another and results in an extreme form of individualism, which encloses each person within themselves, within their own reality.

Terms like *freedom, independence, autonomy, free expression, self-determination* and so many others are no more than synonyms of the process of separatism. Today nations are divided into provinces and regions, which claim absolute originality and self-sufficiency. But the process continues, and the regions and provinces continue to be divided up into smaller segments, based on any differences or distinctions that can be shown. The next step will be for one town to become separated from another, and even within the same families we will begin to notice cracks that will inevitably result in clashes between the generations.

When, as the culmination of this process, the individual becomes the ultimate unit and becomes "separated" from all the rest, what will happen then? We will be in the heart of the Middle Ages. Everyone will have to look out for themselves even in the simplest of difficulties, and all the achievements of civilization, founded on collective work and cooperation, will have disappeared.

Perhaps, in the present, we may find it difficult to imagine a world without communications, where roads are cut off, where there is no fuel or energy; it may be almost impossible now to imagine large houses in the middle of the countryside and the great cities abandoned because they have become uninhabitable… But as separateness increases, all of these trends are on the rise.

However, as there have been many other Middle Ages before, and as human beings have emerged from all of them, we will also be reborn from this strange period that awaits us. But to be reborn an awakening is necessary, a firm mind that allows us to recognize the mistakes of the present in order to transform them into future successes.

The human being is a social being. The family, the village

or town, the Earth that witnessed our birth all give rise to feelings of affection that cannot be erased from human nature. Those bonds just need to be strengthened in a healthy way. It is enough to remove the parasites from this plant of civilization, so that the new Middle Ages can pass over us like a fleeting dream and, after that brief hour of rest, the dawn of a new world can re-emerge, powerful and radiant.

New and therefore better.

The Pathology of Fear

We have said it several times before and there is no harm in repeating it: the human being is suffering from the disease of fear and its consequences are growing worse by the day.

Fear is like a terrifying claw which closes in upon us, tearing at our thoughts, feelings and will, and removing all possibility of intelligent action. The activity of life is reduced to defending ourselves, escaping from everything, running away from responsibilities, evading definitions, hiding so as not to attract attention. The grey and the dull are what is most appreciated today and those are precisely the characteristics of fear, which is also dull and grey.

There is a special mode of being that appears in these circumstances: the "anti-" – the person who opposes anything that involves any form of decisiveness. They see everything as bad, because negative aspects are the first ones to be noticed, while their growing fear makes them miss any opportunity of recognizing virtues.

To be against everything – which is the same as not being in favour of anything – is the new pathological expression of fear. The only thing people see as positive is their own advantage, their own survival, even if to achieve that they have to destroy everything else, which is what happens next. This is, evidently, an aberrant form of egoism, in which the "self" asserts itself to such an extent that it despises everything around it. There is no attempt to overcome the evils affecting the world; instead, out of fear, they deny and denigrate, while at the same time hiding their heads beneath the wings of inaction.

The philosopher must eradicate fear, and with it, all its consequences. He must learn to distinguish the good from the bad, he must stand up for his ideas and distinguish them from other opposing ideas, but always using willpower and action. We cannot simply be "anti-"; we have to have, in principle, some firm and genuine ideals of our own if we are to oppose something else. Before rejecting, we have to accept something. Before denying, we have to know something.

The philosopher can find mistakes and flaws in different aspects of life; but he is not content merely to point them out or be afraid of them; he works hard to improve everything that is in his power to change, starting, naturally, with himself.

The philosopher also notices that, in addition to the bad, there is always the good and the positive; it's just that sometimes it lies asleep or buried beneath the waves of fear and inertia. Virtues, like every good plant, must be cared for and cultivated before they can flower.

The philosopher is never against life, but in favour of it; he accepts its treacherous currents and makes an effort to obtain a clarity of ideas that will allow him to navigate successfully through the world. Those who are "anti-everything" will end up becoming anti-human, and the philosopher values the human condition as an indispensable factor for creating the new and better world we all want to see.

Facing Disaster

As the century approaches its end[1], the belief that we are facing a catastrophe seems to find easier and more abundant prey; we are faced with a real fatalism which saps people's energies and makes it more difficult for events to unfold in an appropriate way.

As has happened at other times in history, human beings feel incapable of finding solutions to all the evils that are threatening us and, although it is never publicly recognized, the truth is that discouragement and indifference are gaining ground.

On the one hand, there is the simple apathy of those who are unable to do anything from their humble positions in society. On the other hand, there is the even greater discouragement of those who know that we are only working with hypotheses, not with certainties, about what is going to happen. The lack of decisiveness in confronting the current widespread situation means that the theories about the possible end of the world, about major catastrophes that could occur in the next few years, are becoming more real in people's imagination.

In view of this state of things, it is not a question of sitting down to wait for the disaster that one decade or other may bring, but of calmly analyzing what we can do as human beings.

We do not in any way rule out the influence that the heavenly bodies may have over our planet and, naturally, over

---

1 Editor's note: this was written in 1996, with the year 2000 approaching.

its inhabitants. If the universe is a great living being, with coordinated movements, it is reasonable to assume that all its parts are connected and that the movement of the heavenly bodies is reflected in other kinds of related movements, both on the Earth and among human beings. From this point of view, some catastrophes, which, in any case, have been manifesting for some time, are likely to take place, both as a result of geological movements and the growing aggression among human beings.

But those catastrophes are not determining factors, nor do they imply the end of the world. History has many records of such difficult moments, cataclysms and disturbances, fears and psychoses about a certain end, the outcome of which was that life continued and there were a greater number of problems to solve, but nothing more.

Our mental attitude must be healthy and decisive. As the philosopher-emperor Marcus Aurelius said, "Nothing can happen to you that you are not made by nature to bear." If catastrophes come, we will know how to deal with them. And far from being discouraged by this probability we need, on the contrary, to build up more energy, more knowledge, more willpower, in order to endure whatever may happen in a dignified manner.

Neither catastrophic fatalism nor unconscious optimism. What is needed is a balanced way of being, in which optimism is displayed only in the light of real results and fatalism disappears before our will in action.

We have to learn how to live for the new times.

Reclaiming Courage

The problem of fear among human beings is not new.

For several years now – perhaps more than we dare think – human beings have been losing confidence in themselves, in the destiny that rightfully belongs to them and, as a result, in the destiny of humanity as a whole. History seems totally alien to them and they do not feel like its builders, but its victims. Time is no longer the factor of hope that allows us to move forward with renewed dreams and constant work; now, on the contrary, time is a lethal weapon which destroys human beings and civilizations, which wears everything out beyond any possibility of recovery.

This result was to be expected and we are all suffering it to a greater or lesser extent.

The human being has lost the ability to communicate, which is ironic as we are in the age of communication. No one trusts anyone else, no one risks telling the truth about what they feel and think, let alone wants to confess that sometimes they are not very sure of what they think or feel… Today everything exudes the false confidence of people who are lying, people who are pretending in order to disguise their lack of inner and outer faith.

This is why fear has emerged. Fear of truth; fear of commitments; fear of loyalty; fear of the harm that other people may cause us and even fear of our own unknown reactions.

Because of fear, sacred words are no longer spoken. Because of fear, healthy friendships no longer arise. Because of fear the best ideals die, because no one wants to stand up for them. Fear puts shifty glances in our eyes, makes our gestures meaningless and indecisive, and our words ambiguous and empty, in order not to commit to anything and to allow us to escape from everything…

To this fear of everyday life is now added the even greater fear of the cycles of history. To grow one year older is almost an unlucky omen; to have begun a new decade must certainly bring new misfortunes and complications; to approach the millennium is a sign of some certain catastrophic end… And all this contributes to making human beings feel even smaller within themselves.

It is time to adopt the opposite attitude. Fear is synonymous with weakness and lack of confidence. It is necessary, then, to reclaim our courage: to know ourselves, to know other human beings; to clarify our understanding and return to God and to the truths that are found in Nature.

We should not be frightened by new years or new decades, and all the conjunctions of the stars together should not move by a single inch the firm will of a human being who feels within himself the fire of infinite life.

We are not products of chance floating aimlessly in space. We are the result of a complex chain of causes and effects that ultimately derive from God.

Try it out: look at things in this way and you will lose your fear.

Adopt this new vision and you will become a new human being.

Pain and Suffering

There is a question which, whether silently or out loud, we tend to ask ourselves several times a day - many, too many times in our lives. Why do people suffer? Why does pain exist?

This question points to a reality from which we cannot escape. Everyone suffers; for one reason or another, everyone bleeds in their heart and tries vainly to grasp happiness, which is imagined as an uninterrupted succession of joys and satisfactions.

A parable from Buddhism which has always made an impression on me comes to mind; it is known as "the parable of the mustard seed". To sum it up, it is about the pain of a mother who has lost her child, yet still believes that he can be brought back to life thanks to the magical arts of the Buddha. He does not discourage the mother; he just asks her, if she wants to resuscitate her child, to obtain a mustard seed from a household where no misfortune has been known… The end of the parable is obvious: the mustard seed, that very special seed, will never be found and the pain of the mother will be partly mitigated when she finds out how many and how great are the sufferings of all other human beings.

But the fact that all human beings suffer does not take away or explain the reality of suffering. And once again we ask ourselves: why?

Ancient teachings – more ancient even than the parable referred to above – help us to penetrate the intricate labyrinth of pain.

In general, we are told that suffering is the result of ignorance. Thus, we add one pain on top of another, that is, we add to the painful events themselves the lack of knowledge of the causes that have given rise to those events: we are not capable of reaching the roots of things in order to discover the deep origin of what is troubling us; we simply remain on the surface of pain, at the point where it is felt most acutely and where we feel powerless to get out of the trap. We are ignorant of the cause of what is happening to us and we are ignorant of ourselves, thus creating a double incapacity for positive action.

We are also ignorant of other fundamental laws of Nature, and once again, because of ignorance, we increase our pain. We should know that no pain is eternal, that no pain will be lasting if we apply a constructive will. Nothing, whether pain or happiness, can last forever in the same state. We must learn, then, how to play the game of time in order to find one of the possible ways out of the labyrinth.

The pain of what is to come has no place in the present, since it is a useless suffering, before its time; and there may, after all, be no real reason for it. It is true that in the present we are already creating the future, but it is also true that fear of the future is the seed of future evils, while a firm and positive will gives rise to more favourable circumstances which can also be created in the present.

The pain we feel for things past is like trying to keep the corpse of a beloved person in our house, constantly repeating to ourselves that he or she has not died, looking again and again at the unreality of a body which no longer exists and being unaware of the other spiritual reality which does exist.

As for the pain of the present, it is no more than a short, sharp pain, soon to be consigned to the past, to make room for the future.

That is why a wise man said that we human beings are capable of suffering three times for the same thing: waiting for it to happen, while it is happening and after it has happened. Hence, the view that "ignorance is the mother of all sorrows" is reinforced.

For the Eastern philosophers, following the same line as the Buddhist parable, "pain is the vehicle of consciousness"; which is equivalent to saying that all suffering contains the necessary teaching for our evolution.

Pain is what forces us to stop and question ourselves about things. Without pain, we would never say to ourselves, as we so often do: "Why me?" - and then notice, immediately, that it is not only happening "to me". Without pain, we would not make the effort to go deeply into the hidden laws that move all things, events and people.

Wherever we look, we will find suffering: the seed suffers when it breaks open to allow the tree to come into being; the ice suffers when it melts with heat and so does the water when it hardens with cold; and human beings also suffer when, in order to evolve, they have to break the old skins of their prison of matter.

But hidden behind all these sufferings lies an unknown happiness: the fullness of the seed, of the water, of the human soul. They all discover, in the midst of the darkness, the unwavering light of their own destiny.

Stress

Sometimes, when our holidays come to an end and we have to return to our normal activities, the problems we thought we had left behind on our departure resurface again into the light of consciousness.

One of those problems is summed up in a word which we hear about more and more nowadays: stress.

Work is stressful, study is stressful, as are the obligations we have entered into, the many commitments we have to live up to, the complications we don't know how to solve… It's as if the holidays had been for nothing, as if those few or many days of rest had been wiped out just by thinking about what awaits us.

But do we really know how to rest? Or do we interpret rest as the fact of doing little or nothing, not thinking, assuming a different personality to the one we have during the rest of the year?

That is evidently not the way to rest. It is merely a way of escaping for a brief period of time, of hiding from the pile of things that await us on our return and will make us feel stressed again; we fall into the grip of anxiety and feel trapped by the demands of life, whether real or imagined. We are stressed by obligations and even by rights that we often don't know how to exercise or don't fully understand. We have no other choice but to plunge into the vortex and hope that the months will pass, bringing our next holidays closer, which we imagine will be better than the last ones and will truly give us an opportunity to rest.

But year after year the same story repeats itself.

As we have been taught by the Stoic philosophers, the problem lies within us and not outside us.

It is impossible to get away from our usual worries by travelling, because we will inevitably carry them with us in our suitcase. So there is no point putting a physical distance between ourselves and our problems or letting our minds go "blank". We ourselves become our own enemies and we are the cause of our detested stress. It is not a question of moving from one place to another or planning some rest for ourselves unless we are actively and intelligently part of the process.

Why do we live in a state of stress? In principle because there are too many things we have to attend to within a time that we find far too short. However, as philosophers, we need to ask ourselves how important those things that cause us stress really are. Do they all really deserve to hold such a central position? Is it not possible to make a selection between the things that are really worthwhile, those which are less so and those that are not worthwhile at all?

The most likely outcome of such reflections is that some clarifying answers will arise to resolve the stress that envelops us like an impenetrable mist. We will most probably discover that we are trapped by things – not by their quantity, but by their triviality: doing many things that lead nowhere, constantly on the move without really knowing where we are going, having no defined goals or having goals that are unrealistic. In this way, the inner human being dies under the weight of an absurd, complex and enervating construction, which was supposed to have been made for his own protection, for his personal development.

But it is useless to cover the Self in so many clothes that it disappears. The trivial destroys the higher human being we all carry within us, who needs open windows to be able to express himself. The trivial causes stress, demoralizes us, prevents us from living, from getting tired and resting, because it has its special rhythm of insatiable madness.

A little air and light, in other words, a little healthy knowledge, will open up a way through to the Self which is always present within us, and stress will give way to an unsuspected harmony, in which time, space and energy will act on the basis of the *eternal and essential*.

Aggression

Unfortunately, one of the salient characteristics of human beings in our times is aggression. They explode with anger at any time and at the slightest provocation, whether or not it is justified. Aggression is a force which is always on the point of bursting out, like a torrent of water that is almost out of control, but its causes, though difficult to understand, are still worth studying.

In principle, two typically aggressive ways of being can be distinguished: the type that comes from adults and the type that characterizes young people.

The aggression of adults, although as unpleasant as the other, is perhaps more justifiable. In this case there is an accumulation of dissatisfactions over many years – failures, shattered dreams, dreams that were simply allowed to die… It arises from a rejection of our own past, which we cannot or will not accept, and an apparent fear of the future, which appears uncertain, with nothing desirable to look forward to. Then aggression explodes in the face of everything and everyone, because everyone else is to blame for what each one, individually, was unable to do. A scapegoat has to be found, and it is always better if the propitiatory victim is someone other than ourselves.

In the case of young people, aggression is a mask that covers many conflicting situations. Young people are energetic by nature and need to apply their energy to something; if they find a way of directing it intelligently, they become fulfilled human beings; if they fail to find a way of expressing all that energy, they turn it against others and against themselves under the form of aggression.

It has often been said that young people have their whole lives ahead of them, and it is true; but what lies ahead of them does not offer them any security. Nor do they know with any certainty whether they are going forward, or whether they are simply going somewhere. They don't trust the preceding generations, but they don't dream of the coming generations either, and at the same time they have great difficulty in putting up with those who share their own problems and way of life. Young people feel hemmed in by a set of insecurities – first of all within themselves – and by an accumulation of premature disappointments which inevitably end in despair. The immediate result of this despair is, precisely, aggression. Everyone else is to blame for their disappointment and, when they are tired of blaming and attacking others, they turn against themselves. Hence the abnormal number of suicides that occur among young people; suicides with no apparent cause, but which, nevertheless, have been incubating for a long time in the troubled minds of those who feel "alienated from the world".

For one reason or another, it is our fate to live at a time when there is a lack of harmony between human beings. Aggression has replaced the good sense of wisdom. And let it be clear that we are not referring to violence, which is a more or less direct result of aggression, for that is a different and much more acute problem. Here we are only concerned about that growing bitterness which has become the common denominator of human relations.

There are no quick and easy solutions, because solutions cannot appear from one day to the next and because they need the direct cooperation of all the people involved in a given situation. In any case, the greatest urgency relates to young people, to that generation which, in a not so distant future, will have to take charge of their own destinies and, therefore, of the destiny of their entire age.

It is essential to eliminate the "emptiness", the lack of goals, hopes, plans, studies and work. Young people need to know why they are alive, what they are living for and how they are living. No one will be able to avoid the natural trials and tribulations of existence, but at least there will be a sense of responsibility that will allow them to face with integrity each of the problems that arise.

Once more, philosophy, in its fullest sense as love of wisdom, and in its application as a way of life, presents itself as an appropriate solution to an aggression which, in the best of cases, is no more than a pointless waste of energy.

The mask of aggression will fall when human beings, and young people in particular, can sincerely express their true values, without the need to disguise the emptiness of their hearts, which are suffering because of ignorance.

Fear of Public Opinion

When good sense and knowledge disappear from everyday life, then so-called "public opinion" rises up as an infallible judge of everything that is said and done.

However, public opinion is neither wise nor sensible, not because it is incapable of being so, but because it is not interested. On the contrary, it is all about manipulating that opinion, making it as changeable as fashion itself.

Every day we can see public opinion moving between the two perpetual extremes – praise and blame – swinging from one to another like a constant pendulum. And that pendulum is so powerful that praise is what makes existence and action possible, while blame paralyzes us, making us afraid to raise our heads above the parapet.

The verdict of the court of public opinion is considered so final that many people aspire to nothing more than a state of calm, an inertia in which no one loves or hates us, but no one takes any notice of us either.

However, praise and blame are signs of movement, while the anonymity of tranquillity is a sign of immobility. If we do nothing, we risk nothing, and as a result we don't enter the game of extremes by which we are either accepted or rejected. If we act, we must accept as logical and natural that there will be those who are in agreement with our action and those who are not. But this should not stop us from acting, because those who are convinced of the need for action do not care about praise or blame; they only care about fulfilling their duty, regardless of what public fashion may think about duty.

History, in its constant unfolding, shows us that in its different cycles there are different human interests: sometimes duty and honour are more important than anything else, and sometimes these principles are eclipsed by a hedonism and a materialism that are not interested in making commitments to the inner human being, to history or to God. This is where "public opinion" and its different fashions come into play. And there lies the risk of getting lost in futile speculation, while awaiting the applause that will never come and missing the good opportunities of acting in a useful and effective way in life.

The important thing is to act, to define oneself, to risk making a mistake, but above all to put our human energy at the active service of ourselves, of other human beings and, ultimately, of God. If we are praised, that's fine; if we are not praised, that's fine as well; and if we are criticized, that's equally fine.

Just as the sun never ceases to shine, nor the sea to crash against the coasts, so, with the same inexorability, and beyond mere opinions, the idealistic human being must fulfil his destiny, giving space to the voice of his old and deep consciousness, rather than to the versions that change with time.

> "Before the soul can hear, one has to become as deaf to roarings as to whispers, to cries of bellowing elephants as to the silvery buzzing of the golden fire-fly." (*Book of the Golden Precepts*, Tibet).

Is it Worth it?

We often ask ourselves what is worth experiencing in life, because we frequently come across the well-worn expression, "it's not worth it". It's as if life has put us in front of a well-stocked shop window in which we have to choose between the things we find attractive and those we don't.

There is something in that. And it is interesting to find that, whatever we choose, it will always imply hardship and effort; it's just that some things are worthwhile and others are not.

What, then, is worthwhile today?

Many people think that the first priority is to make a nice life for oneself in the here and now, to have comfort and material possessions. The next step would be to achieve a pleasant vagueness as regards feelings and ideas; because to feel or to think deeply only brings complications which, of course, don't help to relieve the hardships of life. In general, it is more attractive to allow ourselves to be swept along by the current, adapting to accepted opinions, filling the empty hours with emptiness, so that we don't notice that they are empty. Vocation, inquiry, self-knowledge, love, friendship… Such things are no longer fashionable, they are not worthwhile, they don't pay in a society which gives them very little value.

But, if we reflect a little more, we will find that there are things that have always been worthwhile and continue to be so: they are the things that endure, that don't disappear quickly, that accompany us both today and tomorrow.

* It is worthwhile getting to know ourselves as conscious human beings, because whatever we learn in this sense will certainly endure and no one will be able to take it away from us.

* The closer we come – whether by reason or intuition – to the important truths of life, in the sense of stable and substantial ideas, the more confidence we will have in ourselves, and that is certainly worthwhile.

* The more we know ourselves and understand people and their problems, the more affection and friendships we will have and, even if they are not lasting in all cases, this is also worthwhile.

* By dedicating our life to an occupation that is useful to ourselves and others we give meaning and purpose to existence, and that is also worthwhile because it lasts as long as our years on Earth.

All these and more are lasting elements which we can find in the philosophical traditions of all times and places. And this is something that is worth living: *Philosophy understood as a way of life.*

Knowledge or Wisdom?

A few centuries ago Francis Bacon stated that, for some people, the purpose of knowledge is merely to gratify their curiosity. And more recently a great teacher added that Bacon's statement was similar to that of earlier philosophers who highlighted the distinction between wisdom and knowledge.

The dissemination of knowledge in all its branches, whether scientific, philosophical, artistic, sociological, political or economic, and so many others that do not come to mind at present, has resulted not so much in a serious diffusion of knowledge as in the creation of a market intended to satisfy people's curiosity. And if there is no curiosity, then someone will appear to promote it using sensationalist advertising and the wide and indiscriminate use of the mass media.

It goes without saying that curiosity is never satisfied by these means, because the public – in most cases – is not prepared to study such a wide variety of topics in any depth and because those who practise the above-mentioned disciplines – and others we may have forgotten to mention – change their positions and opinions as quickly as they discover or believe they are discovering new aspects in the fields of their research. Which means that there will be plenty of subjects to awaken curiosity for a long time…

But let us go one step further. Let us go from simple curiosity to a kind of knowledge that is developed and deepened over years of study and work. Although this may seem to be the highest attainable goal, that is not the case either, because this type of knowledge only relates to a specific part of the person:

depending on the cases, it occupies the mind, the body or the feelings, but it is rare for it to open the imposing gates of intuition, the hidden aspects of the soul, the unstoppable desire for perfection, whatever the task we have undertaken.

It is here that we enter the domain of wisdom. To be wise is much more than to know. Wisdom is a kind of knowledge that we never forget, that is not simply rooted in the outer surface of memory, but in the deepest folds of true being. What is known with wisdom becomes a part of ourselves. And just as our Self always "is", even if it is not the same as a child or as an adult, wisdom obliges us to become more mature with time, although time becomes eternal when it relates to our own growth.

We are in an age of great conquests. Everyone claims to offer us the best. So let us demand the best and let us begin by demanding it of ourselves. Whenever we act, whatever we look at, whatever we feel or think about as we go about our daily lives, let us do so with a spirit of greatness and perfection; with a vision which, by its sheer breadth, brings together sciences, arts, religions and philosophies as part of a single family.

Our field of action is WISDOM.

The Need to Stand Out

Let us ask ourselves about one of the aspects that is most important for the human beings of our times: what are the different ways of achieving success, of standing out? There is one thing that is indisputable: all human beings, in one way or another, try to stand out, to succeed; it is like a vital necessity. It is the need to do something, but above all, something important; it is the need to act, but to act in a way that does not pass by unnoticed. It is about "being someone", not disappearing into anonymity, ensuring that our name will be on the lips of the greatest possible number of people.

The natural law of life leads us to act. The whole universe acts, moves, is going somewhere, even if we cannot say exactly where. So the need for action should not surprise us, since the human being responds harmoniously to the universal laws. It is also natural that every action should have results, a response that is in accordance with the action. But today, action and its results are seen under the lens of easy success: the important thing is to excel, to stand out from others, rather than ensuring that the things that we do are done well; as long as they look as if they have been done well, that is enough.

In this unstoppable race to stand out, we can find different forms of action.

* There are those who make a personal effort and, within their possibilities, seek some appropriate means of standing out.

* Others also rely on their own effort and work, but do not focus on the means that will lead them to obtain those desired outward signs of success.

* And there are plenty of people who simply set about crushing others in order to seem taller themselves.

In one way or another, the results that are obtained, with some exceptions, are rather sad. The required condition of outer success produces dissatisfied human beings in the best of cases, or traumatized and neurotic ones; there are many others who are depressed, envious, brutal and aggressive, or vain, cruel and ruthless, without excluding the social climbers and opportunists and hundreds of other examples that would expand the above-mentioned fauna.

Let us ask ourselves, then: where is this race leading and what is its purpose? History, as the experience of humanity, and our own personal experience both indicate that all this glitter comes and goes with the wind. What is valid today is stigmatized tomorrow and what would have been subject to the death penalty yesterday is admired today.

Who do we want to stand out among and for what purpose?

This question that I am asking leads me to think that the desire to stand out is a natural impulse of the soul: it is natural for the human being to aspire to ever more and better things. But I also understand that to excel is essentially to grow, to truly grow, not to wear stilts; it is to stretch oneself inwardly to the highest and best point within ourselves. And it is to earn our own self-respect, our self-esteem, it is to be at ease with our own conscience.

There are ways of standing out that seem to be almost forgotten now, such as, for example…

* Knowing ourselves so as to better control our negative aspects and strengthen the positive;

* Taking as models, without any false modesty, those who have been able to succeed in the name of the good, the beautiful and the just;

* Forgetting about the demands of fashion or the psychological and pseudo-rational madness of a particular moment;

* Making life an exercise of daily self-improvement…

It is appropriate to remember that it is not good to stand out just for a moment, because this would lead to the same states of despair as are experienced by those who have not achieved the necessary symbols of prestige. On the other hand, it is worth making a serious and sustained attempt that will lead us to a solid, stable, uninterrupted inner growth, always in search of the greatest and the best.

That is why we asked ourselves about the need to stand out and the purpose of doing so; and about the means that exist to achieve it.

The need is clear. The purpose and the means depend on the choice which each person is able to make. In this case, there will never be too many questions to ask ourselves if we ask them as sincerely as possible.

What is Inspiration?

This is a question that arises when we think of real masterpieces, those creations and performances of genius which some human beings have managed to produce, as if they had been directed by special powers, which seem to have come from some source above the artists themselves. What was the magic spark that guided them? What extraordinary streams of thought or vision were they able to follow?

That too is the question that torments us personally in those moments when we want to express the best of what we feel and think, but don't know how to do so. It is also what we ask ourselves when we feel empty of ideas and emotions, as if we were a lifeless bag of skin and bone.

Then we remember the great creators, those who were able to enter into contact with inspiration by briefly touching its secret. Is it possible to know for certain that there is a bridge between human beings and the world of ideas, capable of establishing the link that we call inspiration? Perhaps there is not just one bridge, a single link between us and that world; because if that were the case, those who have been able to cross the bridge would have told us how they did it and what it was like when they reached the other side. Perhaps each human being has to cast their own nets, with their own means, and therein lies the mystery of the awakening of inspiration.

From another point of view, I fear that the rational mind, which we have made the distinctive symbol of the human being, has little or nothing to do with this process.

Experience tells us that the more we try to achieve this state with our reason, the further away we get from inspiration.

The ancient sages used to say that the secret lies in becoming like a hollow reed… and allowing intuition to flow through it. It is then that the miracle occurs: we continue to be empty – hollow, more than empty – and a procession of images parades before us, obliging us to act extraordinarily quickly. What is not said, painted, written or produced in that instant will be lost. It is not a question of works that are our own exactly; something or someone gives them to us, and our task is to receive and transmit them. It is a moment of ecstasy, of contact with a world which is different to our own, more ethereal, more beautiful, more perfect in all its aspects. It is like having a highly sensitive receiving device, which we don't know how to use and operate. We can only make use of it when it is working.

We have several descriptions – some more inspired and others less so – which give us a possible key of interpretation. If there is an affinity between our personal vibrations and that world of perfect ideas that we want to reach, the contact is established just by desiring it strongly. It is up to us, then, to develop and nourish those streams of sympathy that are in accord with the good and beautiful aspects we want to understand and transmit. It is up to us to open the doors to inspiration.

And when we ask ourselves again, "what is inspiration?", it is likely that we will still not have a definite answer; but we will, on the other hand, have the strange and marvellous sensation of having been touched by a wonderful aura that comes from beyond time and space, from the eternal source from which all of us, at some time, have dreamt of drinking.

Why do Feelings get Worn Out?

Sometimes it is interesting to return to questions we asked ourselves when we were taking our first steps on the path of a philosophical ideal; above all, so that we can check the answers that experience has given us and be sure that the spirit remains unchanging in its fundamental concepts.

Years ago, I used to get upset by the certainty with which "adults" would predict that my highest dreams, my aspirations to live a different, better and deeper life full of meaning would not last long. They told me – it was me then, and I fear that many others in a similar situation today are told the same – that ideals are good for providing meaning in our adolescent years, for lighting the first fires that will impel us into the world of action. But later, life with its demands, its repetitions and disappointments, would do its work of erasing those ideals and making way for more practical and realistic systems.

In those times I rebelled against such assertions, and I continue to do so today. Before, I opposed them with the force of my youth, while today I do so with the support of my own experiences, which have proved to me that what seemed like well-established laws laid down by the previous generations were not so well-established after all. There are, however, still some facts that leave the old questions in place. Not all idealists who in their youth want "to take on the world" continue the struggle with the same force as time passes. Why do ideas and feelings become worn out? What happens to those who allow the best parts of themselves to die along the way?

Today, the answer I give myself is that only that which is of a perishable nature can become worn out. It is logical that all material bodies gradually lose their suppleness and that energy, which is another form of matter, gradually leaves them. That is a law inherent in all manifestation in this objective world. But, as we enter the more subjective planes of the human being, such as ideas and feelings, where we no longer have to rely on the support of matter, can we not achieve a more lasting quality?

I would never aspire to an absurd immobility or the fossilization of mental and emotional structures with no room for variation. No. Just as bodies gradually adapt to the needs of life, which uses them to express itself, so too, ideas and feelings can change with time. But the aim should always be to achieve greater perfection, a weeding out of unnecessary elements on the basis of experience; not to disappear like dust, to get worn out like a pair of very old shoes, to become like leaking boats or walls full of holes…

Let us ask ourselves, then, about the quality of those feelings and those ideas that have perished before the onslaughts of time. Surely, then, they were as fragile as the matter of the body, or even more so, since they have not lasted as long as the life of that body? Are they not just daydreams, mirages, barely even shadows, which some people cling on to in ignorance for a moment, only to collapse later on when the passing illusion is shattered by disappointment?

And yet, we could ask ourselves about other examples, which are the exact opposite of the ones we have just mentioned. What is the nature of those feelings that transcend the barriers of life and death, that reappear again and again with the same perseverance as the sun which rises again every morning? What can we say of those firm ideas that inspire a whole existence and which are solid enough to continue to inspire other human beings? What can we say of the scientists who research and work tirelessly, inheriting aspirations and efforts from one another, until they achieve their goals? Of the mystics who love God in all things and above all things? Of the Romeos and Juliets, the Parises and Helens, the artists perpetually in love with their art, the philosophers, tireless followers of the timeless wisdom?

Are there not, then, some solid, enduring, exemplary elements on the inner planes? Of course there are, of course they are possible! We just have to know how to find them, not to allow ourselves to be deceived by false arguments or allow ourselves to fall when faced with the trials of life. Nothing valuable is ever achieved without effort, and no feeling or idea which is valid enough to direct the whole of our path in life can come to us ready-made, without conquest or struggle.

That which becomes worn out bears the mark of the fallible within itself. Let us allow it to get worn out, then; let it follow its destiny. On the other hand, let us try to preserve what we know can be a treasure and support for the whole of our life, for all our lives. Let us know how to ask ourselves every day about how solid our experiences really are, and let us also know how to strengthen everything that nourishes us spiritually. Let us build worlds of ideas and feelings that can remain with us for all of our time, and even longer, so that we can reencounter them when the time comes – as it comes for all things – to begin again and to recognize ourselves.

The Everyday Hero

Among the many things that are out of fashion at the moment is the heroic sense of life. Heroes are something for books, not even for history books, but fantasy stories for children, who are entertained with paper or celluloid heroes, as long as the psychologists don't intervene to declare that such tales are bad for their minds.

In spite of such fashions, however, life in its rich variety offers us many more heroic deeds than we are often prepared to admit. I am not talking about the great historical figures, those who, in spite of the cloudy vision of envious critics, continue to shine with their own light in time; no. I am talking about the small everyday heroes, who carry out real feats, with an effort worthy of titans, even if they have the stature of human beings.

Everyone has their own level. Everyone has their own feelings and ideas, their dreams and ambitions. Everyone has some desire to change, to improve, to leave the world a little bit different from the way they found it… And it is there, in that part of each individual, with all those characteristics, that the everyday hero is to be found, laboriously striving to achieve a part, whether great or small, of all that we have mentioned.

If some talented writer were to record the adventures of these anonymous people and give them expression in words, he would transform those people and their adventures into heroes and heroic deeds, because he would know how to bring out the value of each experience, the heroic act of each minute.

When classical philosophy imagined the heroes and made them recognized by all, I believe that their vision was not only based on warlike deeds or outstanding acts of psychological or physical skill. I think I can glimpse, in more than one philosopher, a silent and subtle invitation to emulate those heroes from the simplicity of our own lives, from the battle station in life which destiny has assigned to each one of us.

The heroic sense of life is not only to be found on the battlefield, or at one of those difficult moments when we have succeeded against all odds. The heroic sense of life and the single act of heroism are not the same. The heroic sense of life is like a general direction; it is a path which, passing through more or less difficult terrain, leads to a goal.

Heroism, then, consists in seeing each day, each act, as a test or trial in which all our strengths - from physical strength to the subtle powers of intelligence and the soul – are going to come into play. Sometimes we will fall, and many other times - as many as may be necessary – we will get up again… Maybe you don't yet feel the hero in yourself? Make space for him and you will see him grow like an inner column.

This is an invitation to the heroic: to be different, to be better, to be clear, honest and reasonable in the name of a natural philosophy, when everyone seems determined to harm themselves for the sake of pretentiousness and ignorance.

Criticism

Although there are many people who have spoken on many occasions of constructive and destructive criticism, we venture to dissent in this respect, since daily experience shows that criticism is always destructive. And this is not the fault of criticism as a rational process, but of the people who act under the guidance of their emotional and subjective impulses rather than reason and common sense.

We live in a world that wears a mask of confidence and certainty, but it is the opposite that lies deep within each human being where insecurity, doubt and fear are evident to a greater or lesser extent.

On the one hand, the potential for action and creation has been significantly reduced; on the other, the ability to understand and overcome problems has been restricted by the ignorance that exists in these fields. As a result, people protect themselves, disguising their fears and their incapacity under the form of criticism.

In general, everything becomes an object of destructive criticism, because the worse other people are made to appear, the better others feel when unconsciously defending themselves by concealing their own defects.

The critic is automatically the one who knows, who can supposedly do things better than others and has the solutions to all problems.

The critic never tries to look for anything good in anything or anyone, never tries to find justifications for any mistake and never forgives the slightest failing.

The critic is, therefore, the one who thinks he is in possession of the whole truth and considers himself to be free from all mistakes; at most, he will save his praises – which will be more or less expansive according to the needs of the case – for the person, group or sociopolitical structure in which he feels protected.

The critic, in any case, will be very wary about putting his ideas into practice, because by putting something into practice he risks becoming the object of the same or worse criticisms as he has applied to others. Criticism generates criticism; ill will only gives rise to more ill will.

This does not mean we should close our eyes, ears and mouths and allow anything to pass, even if we genuinely consider it to be wrong. But we believe that there are ways of pointing out mistakes and ways of turning the critical spirit inwards in order to improve ourselves, in a way that would, at least, bring something good out of that criticism.

Despite the deliberate lies which are foisted upon us by the diabolical system of life we are currently leading, the fact is that there are still men and women of good will in the world; there is nothing more beautiful than recognizing the achievements of such people and supporting them.

And it is equally true that, if we cannot find anything worthwhile, there is no better form of constructive criticism than to start working on whatever we believe to be good and possible. *Personal example is still the best of teachings*, the best demonstration and the most complete argument.

Symbolic Language

Centuries before the media launched the ideas of psychoanalysis onto the market, it was well known by the sages of antiquity that human beings express themselves through symbols and that their behaviour can generally be interpreted with deeper keys than superficial appearances might suggest.

And although there is nothing new in this, what should be new is the need to understand what these symbols mean, since they affect us all to a greater or lesser degree.

Today, more than ever before, the difficulties of life require us to use a symbolic language; the fear of loneliness and of being misunderstood forces us to hide most of our feelings and ideas or, at least, to find suitable disguises for them. So we have the skills needed to decipher this form of expression which is gradually turning into a new language.

Today, as at many other times in history, human beings are attempting to live in the present minute by minute, denying any significant value to the past and trying to forget about the future. As a symbol, this forgetfulness of the past may indicate several possibilities: from ignorance to a misdirected desire for renewal; from fear of comparisons to the other fear of not being able to live up to the demands of the present. To erase the past is therefore the best way of giving more value to the little or nothing that is being done in the present.

But much more dangerous is the disregard for the future. Here it is indeed worth trying to unravel the symbols that are hidden behind that negative attitude. It is difficult for thinking and intelligent beings to free themselves from time and its dimensions; it is difficult, almost impossible, to separate the present from the past and the future. And it is even more difficult not to be interested in the future, when it is there that all the dreams and hopes which inspire us today can be realized.

It is likely that, in symbolic terms, what we most deny is what we are most worried about; what we most despise is what most obsesses our mind and our emotions.

To live only in the present instant would, in this case, be a way of escaping from the fear of facing a future that is not desired but feared, as we know subconsciously that we cannot expect a future that is unaffected by the consequences of what we are sowing now, day by day.

The confusion of our times could give rise to some unpleasant fruits, so we close our eyes to them and imagine that if we can't see them, they are not really there. But the future is inexorable, as is the past, which has already taken place and can never be erased, however much we may paint it in different colours.

As philosophers, as lovers of truth, we have the difficult but noble task of opening our eyes, facing reality and going within, while at the same time building in the present. There is always time to correct the direction of our journey and its objectives; to plan new conditions for the future.

Symbolic language is also relevant in this case, because a healthy optimism about the future produces a powerful impetus that allows us to undertake the most difficult enterprises.

To deny is a symbol of fear. To accept and to make our best efforts is a symbol of *consciousness*.

Being Free

The recent history of humanity seems to have been focused on the appreciation of freedom as one of life's most important treasures. Consequently, everyone is fighting their own battle to win that prized trophy. Everyone wants to be free, but not everyone seems to think that the gift of freedom must be used.

The spectacle that presents itself to us nowadays is similar to that of the gold-diggers of other times, with one marked difference: I fear that those who were searching for gold knew why they wanted it and had thought of a thousand ways of applying it if they should find that coveted metal. Today, on the other hand, almost no one knows why they want freedom; at most, they will tell us that it is so that they can "do whatever they like". But a freedom which is simply free, in the sense of an anarchy empty of content and purpose, follows the example of the miser who desperately accumulates wealth while living in poverty. No miser is capable of explaining either why or for whom he is storing up his fortune; he is simply dominated by the desire for possession.

This is the problem we are experiencing at present: everyone wants freedom, everyone demands it for themselves and for others, but no one dares to use it, let alone allows others to use it. No one dares to commit themselves in a free decision that will be lasting and stable; no one wants to risk their vaunted freedom for anything or anyone. Freedom is a rarely applied item of value, which is usually expressed in nothing more than shouts and protests, although it can end in violence against those who have a different concept of what it means to be free and what is implied by the free exercise of will.

Noble ideals, dignified ways of life, elevated sentiments, faith in God and in the destiny of human beings do not seem to be objectives that apply to freedom. Today it is believed that the freest person is, precisely, one who lacks all those values; now it is maintained that fidelity to a sentiment or an idea limits one's freedom. In this way, freedom is restricted to a lukewarm search for certain elements that will help one to live a comfortable life, but without any commitment; it is all about being free to change, but without taking any risks, either in the changes themselves or in the doubtful moments of stability.

We live in a world of free human beings, who are free as long as they are not doing anything. But that inactive freedom hides the terrible reality of slavery, mainly under the chains of fear, indecisiveness and the inability to choose and live ideas, feelings and actions that are worth the willing sacrifice of that freedom, once it has been effectively won and exercised.

We live in an age of poor misers who die of hunger within sight of their own treasures, who prefer despairing anguish to spending a single coin of their freedom. And the fact is that, once again, the materialistic point of view has led us into the error of judging all things equally. Freedom is not a heap of gold which decreases as it gets spent, but, on the contrary, it is a human condition, a virtue of the soul that grows with constant application.

Yes, we may make a mistake when we commit ourselves. But who can assure us that we are not making a mistake when we avoid all commitments? And is it not the characteristic of freedom to recognize the mistakes we have made and to correct them once they have been recognized?

Classical philosophy has taught us that freedom is a gift that belongs to those who know and master themselves. Such people do not shy away from action or self-sacrifice, but grow with every experience and become freer the more they grow.

This is the valuable contribution of philosophy in the no less valuable *search for and conquest of individual and collective freedom.*

Time

Time... that strange dimension from which we human beings cannot escape, has a wide range of expressions. Its rich variety allows us to live comfortably within it, even while knowing that we are trapped in its nets.

There are many ways in which time can be measured and chronological time is only one of them. For our heart, for our intelligence and for our spirit, on the other hand, there are such different modes of perception of time that we almost seem to be moving in another dimension.

There are, of course, short periods and long periods of time: a time for doing the everyday and immediate things and a time for the grand human achievements, those that relate to the future.

The short-term time can be measured by our watches and is marked by the progressive wearing out of our bodies. The long-term time not only does not wear out, it enriches the soul, bringing it into contact with the idea of eternity.

What is the time in which human beings have to live? Considering the variety of human possibilities, we have to live in all of them, finding the right measure for each of our planes of expression.

Every day something can and must be done in time. Every day small or big problems arise that need to be – or begin to be – resolved. Every day there is a useful new experience to be gained. Every day one can grow a little more within those brief limits set by the hours and minutes.

However, real human activity does not end – or begin here. Beyond the everyday plans and their fulfilment, man, as an immortal being, must set other long-term goals for himself which therefore require a long-term approach.

More time is needed, more ability to take our dreams forward, more faith in a future which, even though it is not yet visible, can be sensed with the more inner and subtle senses we possess.

One time does not get in the way of the other. The present time with its everyday vision does not prevent us from having a vision of the infinite, because in the human being there are both objective aspects and metaphysical aspects; each of them has its own time, its own way of working, its own way of achieving results, its own way of waiting. In the short-term time, waiting is called patience; in the long-term time, waiting is called faith.

Just as we see it as natural that some plants require more time than others to develop, so there are human goals that can be achieved in a few days, while others take years to come to fruition, so many years that we will not be there to enjoy their fruits when they arrive. But that doesn't matter.

If we are truly conscious of our immortality, those dreams that will become reality a long time in the future will still bear within them the stamp of our efforts, and the human beings who will be able to enjoy those achievements in the future will also bear the unmistakable stamp of a humanity that is progressing, a humanity in which fraternity will be a constant seed, both for the time which is measured in minutes and for the time which is measured in centuries.

Eros, Love

What is love? This question is as old as humanity itself. How can we find the now wingless love in the midst of the many varied versions that are presented to us today?

In principle, it might seem that the meaning of love has been enriched to unimaginable limits, offering more and more possibilities of expression. But after a brief analysis, things appear less clear.

Can we call love the ordinary coming together of bodies, so praised by liberal customs? Or perhaps we will call it the frequent changes and exchanges required by the sated and weary instincts of young and not so young people, who no longer find any interest or attraction in anything? Is love the great quantity of aberrations with which people attempt to cover the lack of genuine feelings - in a word, the emotional void?

Does the word "love" cover commercial transactions, short-lived relationships, bonds that become untied at the first sign of difficulty? And what can we say of the progressive loss of enthusiasm, which begins with indifference and ends in hatred? Can there be forgetfulness and indifference where once there was love?

Eros remains silent before my questions. He just stares at his broken wings... And, from the roots of what were his bright feathers a drop emerges, a mixture of blood and tears of unknown origin. In that drop I see the reflections of old images, which oblige me once again to ask about love...

I miss that powerful feeling that lends brightness to the eyes of those who have it and illuminates everything it touches with the same force. I want to re-encounter the limitless enthusiasm of lovers who experience the world as if it existed only for them, who scorn obstacles and feel capable of defeating all monsters.

What has happened to the love that brings happiness, silent ecstasy, a feeling that the heart will burst because it is too small to contain it?

Where are the man and the woman who offer each other everything they have before asking for anything? Where are those who know how to forgive, to wait, to trust, to help, to understand, to look beyond bodies which are destined to grow old? Where is the glorious certainty of having found the being we need to complete our journey through the world?

Where has that rich and expressive language without words disappeared to, the language of those who share the same dream, an identical hope? Where are the thoughtful gestures, the love of beauty, the delicate homage, the continually renewed gratitude of one who loves and knows that he or she is loved? Where is the romantic passion that makes the human being a god far more powerful than his mere instincts?

Where are they now, the lovers who achieved the miracle of stopping time, obliterating space and frightening away death itself? Where can we find those who have made an altar of their union, their devotion, their fidelity and sincerity?

Eros still does not answer. And yet, he holds the key to my questions. He too is travelling through the world looking for beings to inspire with that feeling which is the reason for his existence. And it may be that those beings are much closer than either he or I, with my questions, suspect.

Here and there, wherever we look, there may be men and women who, without daring to confess it, are looking for the god of love. Because when those who experience the indescribable peaks of such an elevated emotion become many, Eros will regain his wings and fly once more through the ether, encouraging and protecting the love of all those who love.

Mistrust

In addition to the many illnesses that are destroying people's already diminished state of health, there are other psychological diseases which, just because they are more intangible, do no less harm than the strictly physical ones.

Mistrust is a corrosive substance that is advancing in our societies, destroying every form of harmonious coexistence, from the most complex forms in large human groups such as political entities, to the family unit and personal relationships.

We cannot compare mistrust with pure evil, nor with deliberately wicked intentions; on the contrary, it is an attitude that assumes bad intentions in others, something which is unfortunately justified by events on too many occasions.

In this respect, we find two radically opposing positions, although both of them result in similar outcomes: the completely gullible person and the totally suspicious person.

The person who does not mistrust others sets out from the basis that everyone is good until proven otherwise. This tends to result in some very beautiful experiences, since the person's very form of being attracts others who think and act in a similar way. But this person also receives tremendous disappointments which oblige them to see life in terms of the "law of the jungle"; as a result, they feel they have to fight their way through life, sometimes hitting below the belt in the process; and even if they would prefer not to have to take part in the system, they find themselves limited to the option of either hitting or being hit, with no other alternative.

The person who mistrusts everyone, on the other hand, saves himself some painful situations, but loses many other opportunities of finding good things. This person sets out from the principle that everyone is bad until proven otherwise; such people are the ones who take the initiative in the "law of the jungle", which means hitting others or running away before they can be hit themselves.

In short, either everyone is good or everyone is bad until proven otherwise… But the fact is that it is much easier to muddy clear water than to clean up muddy water: mistrust muddies everything and it is very difficult to restore the waters to their natural transparency. It muddies and distorts facts, or loses the ability to see them properly, like someone trying to use a muddy stream as a mirror in which to look at themselves.

The final outcome of this widespread situation of mistrust is a terrible injustice in human relationships, where people end up lashing out blindly at one another for no reason or with no need to do so. It all ends in a sad loneliness, in a war of all against all, although it is covered up and disguised behind some polite but false manners. The final destination on this journey is fear, which is one of the masks of mistrust.

Once again, let us ask ourselves about the solution to these questions that life raises. We believe, as we have maintained so many times, that it is about developing common sense, a good dose of discernment, which has been tested over time by exercising our own consciousness and educating our own personality. Only in this way can we trust or mistrust in the right proportion, based on what our now well developed, healthy and stable judgement has told us. It is a question of looking for this formula, not only as a palliative for mistrust, but also for fear which, like the shadow of mistrust, darkens so many lives.

Let us ask ourselves questions and let us learn to answer our own questions. It is worth attempting this inner dialogue because it will significantly improve our dialogue with others.

What we Love and What we Fear

An old teaching, which, being philosophical, is esoteric, says that all of us, sooner or later, encounter what we love and what we fear in life.

Is this perhaps a fateful prophecy, an unavoidable prediction? No, it is a profound teaching, the fruit of a wisdom which is still fully relevant today. It tells us of the evident power that is to be found in our psychological world: the force of the emotions – what we want, what we fear – is capable of pulling the hidden strings of the will; it can coordinate ideas and result in the materialization of real events.

It also presents us with another evident truth: we all go through life full of longings, dreams and aspirations, and we all carry within us, in a more or less hidden way, a certain number of fears.

It is fashionable today "not to be afraid of anything", or rather, to claim that there is nothing to be afraid of. But it is fear that makes us talk openly about our pleasant aspirations and avoid all reference to fears.

Not to be afraid of anything is an extreme danger which is characteristic of the foolhardy and unconscious person. And the claim that there is nothing to fear forms part of the same unconsciousness. To be afraid of everything and all things is a feature of the pusillanimous person, who lacks strength and is the closest thing to a coward.

The best way is the middle way, the inner courage that knows how to recognize things for what they are and to give them their true value. The valiant man knows what he should fear and avoid, and what he should want and strive for.

In conclusion, we all want something, we all fear something, and that is why we will bring both things into being.

The best thing would be for fear to become a healthy fear of the things we should avoid and an incentive to avoid the dangers we can detect and foresee by using our intelligence.

The best thing would be for love to aspire towards increasingly positive goals, so that we can stop producing all the disasters that currently afflict us and so that love can end up occupying the space previously occupied by our fears.

The more we know how to love, the less we will have to fear.

A Fulfilling Life

To speak of a fulfilling life requires us to ask ourselves the question: what is life? For a philosopher, what does it mean to live?

The particular form of existence to which we have been subject over the last few centuries means that certain simple but important values have been forgotten, while their place has been occupied by meaningless elements. That is why it is so difficult to define what life is.

Of course, life is about much more than having a body and attempting to satisfy all its whims, exercising little control over it and ending up as its slave most of the time.

Nor is it about achieving a distinguished position in society, because prestige and praise are illusory shadows that are awarded by human beings who are also part of the illusion; what exists today disappears tomorrow for no apparent reason; those who glorify a certain attitude today deplore it tomorrow with the same passion…

Life cannot be about accumulating power and wealth, because these are subject to the same limitations as praise and blame: they alternate with one another as in a play of light, in which it is almost impossible to recognize anything valid and stable.

We can say the same of someone who places all their hopes on human affections, especially if they don't know how to maintain them and enrich them over time. To raise a family, to perpetuate a name or a tradition, all of that is valuable, but… does it provide a completely fulfilling life? Don't we sometimes feel a deep and hidden longing to ask for "something more", which would give all those other things a new meaning, based on something more valid and significant?

There are those who retreat into their studies, seeking the meaning of existence there; to know is a way of standing out like any other … There are those, on the other hand, who cannot find enough ways of filling the long hours of boredom and seek distractions as a means of escape; nothing is too much to avoid the emptiness of the inner Self, which remains silent before us.

For a philosopher, to live must be much more than all of the above. To live is a school, the most complete and difficult school of all. Body, feelings and thoughts are the tools that help us pass the tests in this difficult, but special stage of learning. Time is the great teacher, and the inner Self is the pupil who gathers experiences throughout the course of existence.

From this point of view, outer circumstances have only a relative value, the value needed to provide us with appropriate situations for our development; but they are not essential or definitive, nor do they make the human being. Moreover, when circumstances are accepted in this way, they cease to become obsessions and can be managed and changed much more skilfully. Only then does the human being begin to become the master of his own destiny.

To live is an act of responsibility towards oneself and others. The philosopher cannot live carelessly; his acts must have a purpose and a logic that can transcend mere physical survival. In the School of Life everything has a reason and, therefore, a means and a purpose.

To live is an act of generosity towards oneself and others. It is about helping oneself and others by learning, and it is about sharing each achievement, each learning experience, making the most of existence by constantly giving to the world in which we find ourselves, and above all by giving to humanity, of which we are a part.

To live is… to be alive. It is not a secret, it is not a play on words. It is to feel part of the living universe and its energies, making the most of them and resonating with them. In this way, the philosopher can make his life an *eternal act*, a movement towards a goal of perfection, which is also eternity.

For the Brave

Now that speaking of virtues is no longer an anachronism and has become a reality and a necessity which is winning over more and more forward-thinking men and women, we want to dedicate some special words to courage. It is true that, in general, courage is in short supply and, in any case, is being dangerously supplanted by aggression, swagger, cynicism and insults. The tyranny of numbers prevails – the gang, society, whatever is "in", what fashion dictates – helped by the insecurity of the weak and timid, who also lack courage.

There is a lack of personal and individual courage, that courage which is born from the deepest part of the human being and is expressed with the greatest serenity.

There is a lack of courage of convictions rooted in the soul, which give self-confidence but without disrespecting others. Courageous people do not base their strength on the weaknesses of others or the approval of majorities; in any case, their own conscience is the majority for them and, backed by that strength, they seek to help those who need them.

Above all, there is a lack of the most outstanding form of courage, which is to face oneself in order to know oneself better, to distinguish between virtues and defects, to reinforce the former and eradicate the latter. There is a lack of courage to be alone with oneself, to drop the false masks and accept oneself as one is, and from there to develop a system of life, a positive action that will lead to what each of us dreams of as good for ourselves and the world.

Based on this criterion, courage is an essential quality of the philosopher, the seeker of wisdom, the one who needs that special spiritual power to open up paths within and outside himself. How can we set out to discover the world and its laws without courage? How can we overcome the trials that existence sets before us without courage? How can we conquer ourselves without courage? In this way, the philosopher applies courage to himself and when he manages to transform it into a well-established part of himself, he displays it in any circumstances that life may present him with, whether as an individual or in relation to other human beings.

This is the challenge that we present through natural philosophy, which is the philosophy of the human being of all times and that of the human being of today: *to develop the courage to be and the courage to know. It is only for the brave.*

The Eternal Seeker

One cannot speak of philosophy without speaking of the philosopher; one cannot mention the world of ideas without speaking of the person who is capable of living those ideas. So, if we had to highlight one of the fundamental characteristics of the philosopher, the lover of wisdom, we would say that such a person has the qualities of the eternal seeker. He is a self-conqueror, who will only stop seeking when he has finally reached wisdom; and we don't know whether, even then, he will go on to seek other things, which are incomprehensible and inaccessible for us today.

The philosopher is like a tracking dog running through fields and forests, over mountains and along the rivers of life, following some very special tracks. He is seeking the real knowledge of all things. He is seeking himself. He is seeking truth. In a word, he is seeking God as the universal root.

But why is his path so long and difficult? Is Truth not to be found in the world in which we live? Can God not be seen here? Is it necessary to cross an infinite desert – our manifested life, our historical environment, our circumstances – to find what we are looking for beyond these frontiers? No.

We believe that God and Truth are to be found in this world, in our environment, in our achievements and in our problems. But they are covered by a thick layer of mud. They are disguised under grotesque figures, to the extent that on many occasions lies occupy the place of Truth and no one seems to be able to unmask them; and inner emptiness and unbelief take the place of the natural impulses of the human spirit.

The skill of the philosopher in search of wisdom lies in finding in the here and now, in the midst of errors and ignorance, in the midst of darkness and traps, those hidden realities that are waiting for the efforts of valiant human beings to bring them to light, so that they can shine with all their power.

It is necessary to search, to search tirelessly, without wasting the slightest opportunity of discovering light in the darkness, of finding some drops of happiness even in the midst of sorrows, a particle of Truth amongst all the confusion.

The important thing is the goal, it is to use the senses and the intelligence as reliable guides to reach it. *A philosopher is someone who knows what they are looking for and how to achieve it.*

We Propose…

We would like to explain once again how we understand and practise philosophy, because to add to the confusion of our times there are many counterfeit copies in circulation, as well as a deliberate unwillingness to distinguish between what is good and bad.

We are living in a period of history which, like many others, has its special achievements and its undeniable evils. To deny the latter is pointless, because it takes away the possibility of finding solutions. To denounce them courageously does not imply pessimism, but rather, common sense. And to act to solve them is the proper course for the philosopher, who puts his thought into practice.

One of the first postulates of traditional philosophy, which we apply in New Acropolis by making it accessible to our times with the appropriate adjustments, is that philosophy is a path for seeking the truth. We are not talking about any absolute truth or definitive dogma, but about making a conscious effort to evolve until we reach, through faith and reason, those first principles that form the basis of our universe. Therefore, neither philosophical ideologies nor the philosophers who follow them are perfect; both are trying to come closer to perfection by making every possible effort. So,

* In the face of false vanity, we propose a natural simplicity, which accepts that mistakes will be made but also acknowledges that great victories can be achieved in the future.

* In the face of deceitfulness and lies, we prefer the truth, although at times it may be hard to express and although on many occasions no one wants to hear it, let alone understand it. Truth radiates a subdued light that does not shine brightly at first, but will prevail in the long term.

* In the face of the cynicism of convenience, we raise the voice of sincerity and purity of heart and mind, even if it brings no apparent benefits.

* In the face of an increasing lack of control in all aspects, which usually leads to unimaginable levels of immorality, we propose a new morality that is not subject to passing fashions, but is based on one's own alert consciousness trained to recognize what is appropriate for the higher and immortal human being.

* In the face of the indifference of many, we recommend a healthy commitment to life and the circumstances of our times, until we feel that we are an integral and engaged part of history.

* In the face of the violence of others, we choose the most human form of strength, which is expressed not only in physical strength, but in the health of the body and in psychological and moral fortitude in the face of difficulties, in serenity and in knowing how to do things well in each moment.

* In the face of growing fanaticism, which has the defect of believing itself to be just and enlightened, we propose eclecticism, the fruit of a long practice of discernment, of measuring and comparing, of choosing after analysis, without ignoring the experiences of humanity, but attempting to overcome failings and difficulties.

* In the face of slander, which tears philosophy to pieces by the easiest means, we choose the courageous and clear expression of ideas, giving each of them their name, even if this requires more time and dedication, which are the means by which philosophers refine their ideas.

* In the face of ignorance, we offer the antidote of wisdom, which is knowledge acquired and applied to one's own life, not as an intellectual adornment, but as a daily and clarifying rule for living, the only one that is effective for awakening us from the lethargy in which we are immersed.

* In the face of pain and helplessness, we propose the acceptance of universal laws, which give real meaning to everything that happens and reduce the sense of powerlessness as we become capable of recognizing ways out of our fears and inner darkness.

* In the face of the absence of ideals and of God, we choose a full life, dedicated to the search for wisdom – because that is what philosophy is – and to the discovery of God behind all valid knowledge.

This is the philosophy of New Acropolis. This is the formula we offer.

Self-Confidence

Self-confidence arises…

* When we know that, to achieve something, it is necessary to take many steps in the same direction, with perseverance.

* When we know that we cannot fight against time; we can only take advantage of the current of time and gain a few minutes in the direction we want to go.

* When we know that it is necessary to clarify our own ideas and feelings, even if it means having to swallow the bitter pill of recognizing ourselves as we are at all times.

* When we know that we are not perfect but are capable of imagining what perfection is.

* When we know that states of mind and feeling are changeable, but that they do not affect the true Self, which is the root of self-confidence.

* When we know that pain is a necessary seasoning in life, indispensable for learning, when sorrows are transformed into experience.

* When we know that action is preferable to inaction and commitment to life is preferable to apathetic indifference.

* When we know that we all have enormous sources of energy that we don't know how to utilize, either because we are unaware of them, or because we don't believe in them,

or because we don't know how to apply them: we need to be measured in our efforts, never holding back and never abusing our own strengths.

* When we know that failures are teachings and successes are trials that have been happily overcome on the path.

* When we know that we will always receive praise and blame, but neither one nor the other is worth as much as what our own serene conscience tells us is positive or negative for ourselves.

* When we know that no one can take away from us our essence as human beings; and that is our strength.

* When we know that living together in harmony with other human beings is wonderful, but we should not wait for others to do everything for us, nor be so proud that we cannot accept any help.

* When we know that if we find people who are better than us, we should take them as examples and not as reasons to feel depressed, and if we find people who are worse, it should show us what to avoid; and we should never be boastful in front of them about what we are and what we possess.

* When we know that as human beings we have a point of departure and a destination to reach; that there is a reason for what we are doing now, a need and a goal.

* When we know that not everything is written down and, for that very reason, we can add a few more words to the Book of Life.

Swimming Against the Current

To swim against the current is…

* To swim upstream when the river is flowing towards the sea.

* To face the waves, knowing that they will dissolve on the beaches.

* To walk straight ahead, with the wind in our face.

* To help Nature when it is being defiled and destroyed.

* To value life when so many of our actions seem to be working in favour of death.

* To regard trees, animals and stones with the same respect as human beings.

* To achieve clean air when it is being polluted.

* To feel free in spite of the many masks of slavery which are designed to deceive us.

* To preserve our own ideas when so many are changing according to fashion.

* To live an ideal when so many are denying everything.

* To search for beauty when so many are despising it.

* To go in search of the Good when so many are trying to

harm others and themselves.

* To care for and protect justice when it is being violated.

* To uphold virtue when vice is being praised.

* To nurture the higher feelings when so many are tending towards the lower passions.

* To be truthful as the best way of confronting falsehood.

* To profess true knowledge wherever ignorance is applauded.

* To preserve common sense in the midst of madness.

* To remain calm when anxiety is spreading all around.

* To live an ideal of fraternity while others are promoting isolation and division. To love peace in the midst of an aggressive world.

* To be courageous in the midst of a weak world.

* To promote understanding between people when so many are closing the doors of their inner Selves.

* To be generous when so many are becoming miserly.

* To cultivate love where hate grows.

* To know how to listen when everyone wants to speak.

* To enjoy silence when noise is taking over everything.

* To value work over idleness.

* To develop willpower over the instincts.

* To persevere in our humanity, in spite of adverse circumstances.

* To have faith when so many are doubting.

* To believe in God when so many deny Him.

* To raise one's eyes to heaven when so many are crawling on the ground.

* To travel with the stars to the beat of the universal rhythm.

In the Classical Tradition

The fundamental difference between what we call philosophy in the classical tradition and the mental and verbal exercise to which philosophy has now been reduced can never be sufficiently emphasized.

In general, there are few today who dare to call themselves philosophers. The study of philosophy has been restricted to a historical survey of the different forms of thought, the authors who upheld them and the occasional argument about the validity of one theory and author or another. The current philosopher is, at most, a good compiler, a recorder of ideas within the chronologically recognised historical context, a critic, a lecturer or a writer who sums up his knowledge.

As we were saying, there are few who undertake philosophy as a way of life and, therefore, of action. There are very few who have the courage and integrity to think freely and to expound their thoughts with complete freedom. The exceptions that exist, even though they are exceptions, are those that still honour philosophy in the classical tradition, the holistic philosophy that is capable of looking deeply at all aspects of life and, furthermore, of looking for human solutions to all the problems that life presents.

The mental and verbal exercise we alluded to above is positive within its limitations. But the human being is much more than a mind that thinks and a tongue that expresses those thoughts with greater or lesser correctness. From the classical – which means traditional – point of view, the simple definition of man as a rational being whose mind distinguishes him from the animals, plants and stones, is not enough. If it were, the human being would have little need for feelings, vitality and the body that serves him as a vehicle. But human nature expresses itself in many different ways and we must give all of them their place, coordinating them intelligently.

This is why we refer to a holistic philosophy, which encompasses the human being in all his possibilities, developing them and harmonising them; a philosophy that allows us to gain a better knowledge of ourselves, of the life we are living and of the universe of which we are a part.

The philosopher must have keys of action to deal with all situations and experiences, keys that are provided by philosophy when it becomes living and all-embracing. And if we don't have the solutions to all problems, we should at least know what a problem is, recognize the unanswered questions, bear the sorrows and learn to live with them.

There is little more, then, that we can write. The rest is a question of practice. *It is up to each one of us to awaken the philosopher we have within ourselves*, to come closer to the knowledge we need and, above all, to become artists and scientists of the complex and wonderful exercise of living.

Delia Steinberg Guzmán

is currently the President of International Organization New Acropolis.

Of Spanish nationality, she graduated in philosophy from the University of Buenos Aires, where she also took courses in exact sciences, journalism and advertising.

A pianist and writer, she is editor-in-chief of the cultural and philosophical magazine *Esfinge* (Sphinx) and a tireless educator, giving courses in symbology, psychology, history of religions, aesthetics, metaphysics, anthropology and many other subjects.

Her books include *The Games of Maya*, *Today I Saw...*, *Someone Told Me That...*, *Philosophy for Living* and various compilations of lectures she has given around the world. All of them have been translated into several languages.

International Organization New Acropolis

New Acropolis is a worldwide non-profit organization, with centres in over fifty countries.

Established by Professor Jorge Angel Livraga on the foundations of practical philosophy and universal fraternity, New Acropolis is inspired by a fundamental respect for human dignity beyond differences of race, gender, culture, religion or socio-economic status. New Acropolis respects diversity but also tries to transcend it in search of a higher unity through shared universal ethical principles.

At New Acropolis, philosophy is more than just intellectual food for thought. We study philosophy as a means to integrate science, arts, ethics and metaphysics in order to work towards global human development.

This vision is implemented through a wide range of programs that combine practical education with cultural and volunteering activities. New Acropolis also promotes an awareness of current affairs, both locally and globally and focuses on improving the human condition by aligning ourselves with the laws of nature.

To learn more about New Acropolis, visit www.acropolis.org